BEFORE USING...

 Before using this book, please read the guidelines inside the back cover. For a free copy of the detailed guidelines go to www.hunterhouse.com or call the ordering number below.

To prevent bleed-through, it is recommended that water-based, rather than spirit-based, markers or pens be used in this Workbook.

MY OWN THOUGHTS AND FEELINGS (FOR GIRLS)

A Hunter House Growth and Recovery Workbook
by Wendy Deaton, M.A., M.F.C.C.
Series consultant: Kendall Johnson, Ph.D.
Illustrated by Marsha Proud

ISBN-10: 0-89793-130-0   ISBN-13: 978-0-89793-130-4

ORDERING INFORMATION

Additional copies of this and other Growth and Recovery Workbooks may be obtained from Hunter House. Bulk discounts are available for professional offices and recognized organizations.

All single workbooks: $11.95   10-pack: $70.00
Workbook Library Special
(one of each workbook—10 total): $75.00

THE GROWTH AND RECOVERY WORKBOOKS (GROW) SERIES

A creative, child-friendly program designed for use with elementary-school children, filled with original exercises to foster healing, self-understanding, and optimal growth.

Workbooks for children ages 9–12 include:

No More Hurt—provides a safe place for children who have been physically or sexually abused to explore and share their feelings

Living with My Family—helps children traumatized by domestic violence and family fights to identify and express their fears

Someone I Love Died—for children who have lost a loved one and who are dealing with grief, loss, and helplessness

A Separation in My Family—for children whose parents are separating or have already separated or divorced

Drinking and Drugs in My Family—for children who have family members who engage in regular alcohol and substance abuse

I Am a Survivor—for children who have survived an accident or fire, or a natural disaster such as a flood, hurricane, or earthquake

I Saw It Happen—for children who have witnessed a traumatic event such as a shooting at school, a frightening accident, or other violence

Workbooks for children ages 6–10 include:

**My Own Thoughts and Feelings (for Girls);
My Own Thoughts and Feelings (for Boys)**—for exploring suspected trauma and early symptoms of depression, low self-esteem, family conflict, maladjustment, and nonspecific dysfunction

My Own Thoughts on Stopping the Hurt—for exploring suspected trauma and communicating with young children who may have suffered physical or sexual abuse

We welcome suggestions for new and needed workbooks

DISCLAIMER

This book is intended as a treatment tool for use in a therapeutic setting. It is not intended to be utilized for diagnostic or investigative purposes. It is not designed for and should not be recommended or suggested for use in any unsupervised or self-help or self-therapy setting, group, or situation whatsoever. Any professionals who use this book are exercising their own professional judgment and take full responsibility for doing so.

You are SPECIAL!

Write or draw your name
in a way that shows how
you are special.

Begin a list of good, SPECIAL things you think about yourself.

_____

_____

_____

_____

_____

_____

_____

_____

_____

_____

Draw a picture
that shows how
you feel
today.

ce.

u feel.

and it's

er

n't

te

or

Who is your favorite
friend? Tell what
you like best about
your friend.

Do you agree ✓ or disag[ree]

- [ ] I am a good person.
- [ ] The world is a good pla[ce]
- [ ] It's okay to say what yo[u]
- [ ] Sometimes parents fight [and it's] okay.
- [ ] It's okay to cry.
- [ ] Parents should live togeth[er]
- [ ] Sometimes people in a fami[ly don't] like each other and it's o[kay]
- [ ] Everyone has a right to pr[ivate] things.
- [ ] Everyone has a right to his [or] her own feelings.
- [ ] It's okay to be sad.
- [ ] It's okay to be mad.
- [ ] Kids have a right to say No [to] adults.
- [ ] Feelings are okay.
- [ ] Growing up can be a good thi[ng]
- [ ] You can help yourself to be [happy?]
- [ ] I deserve to be loved.

Write about the HAPPIEST
thing that ever happened
to you.

What is the most
important thing you
want people to know
about you?

What are some feelings you have felt?

- excited
- unhappy
- lonesome
- mad
- scared
- helpless
- guilty
- sorry
- angry
- stupid
- shy
- loving
- giggly
- silly
- happy
- worried
- confused
- sad

Write any other feelings you have.

_____

_____

©1993 Wendy Deaton and Hunter House Inc.

Complete the following lines:

Something that scares me is

_____

_____

Something that makes me happy is

_____

_____

I feel mad when

_____

_____

I feel sad when

_____

_____

I feel bad when

_____

_____

I feel good when

_____

_____

Draw a picture of your favorite memory.

STORY GUIDE

1. Have your counselor tell a story and you can draw the pictures on the next two pages

OR

2. Write a story and draw the pictures using one of these titles:

- The Little Prince or The Little Princess

- Mom's House and Dad's House

- The Nightmare

- When Wishes Come True

Write or draw about
something that changed
your life forever.

Everyone makes
mistakes. Tell
about a
BIG mistake
you made.

Mistakes are part
of learning
and growing.

What is the most important thing you ever lost?
Remember—what you lost can be a thing, a person, a feeling, an experience, or even something you believed in, like Santa Claus.

Write about a
sad thing that
happened to you.

Write or draw about a scary
thing that happened to you.

Here are some things you can do when you are scared, sad or hurt:

- [ ] ask someone to stay with you
- [ ] ask for information about what bothers you
- [ ] turn on the lights in the dark
- [ ] lock the door
- [ ] play the radio
- [ ] tell someone in your family how you feel
- [ ] tell a friend how you feel
- [ ] cry
- [ ] get a hug
- [ ] play a fun game
- [ ] make hot chocolate

Write some other things you can do that will make you feel better when you are scared:

_____

_____

_____

Write about a time you
got very angry.

Make a list of things you can do when you are angry that are good things to do and that will help you feel better.

Draw a picture
about a dream
you remember.

©1993 Wendy Deaton and Hunter House Inc.

Write about a dream you would <u>like</u> to have.

Write a letter to
someone special and
tell them something
you have not been
able to talk to them
about in person.

Do you agree ✓ or disagree ✗

☐ Love lasts forever.

☐ Love sometimes hurts.

☐ Love is scary.

☐ Love means I'll love only you.

☐ Love means never being jealous.

☐ Feelings of love can change.

☐ Love means never being lonely.

☐ Love means never being selfish.

☐ There are lots of kinds of love.

☐ The more people you love,
the more love you have.

☐ Love means giving to others.

☐ Love means getting from others.

☐ Love keeps growing.

A hero or heroine is someone you look up to because they are brave, smart, strong, or have done something important.

Who is your favorite hero or heroine?

_____

When we try to be like a hero or heroine we can sometimes do our very best.

Name three people you think of as heroes or heroines:

_____

_____

_____

Write what you like about your heroes or heroines. Or, draw a picture of you and one of your heroes or heroines.

If you were going to be in a race, what kind of race would it be?

- [ ] running
- [ ] bicycles
- [ ] cars
- [ ] boats
- [ ] skis
- [ ] skateboards
- [ ] horses

What others?

_____

_____

_____

If you were in a game or sport, what would it be?

- [ ] soccer
- [ ] baseball
- [ ] volleyball
- [ ] football
- [ ] tennis
- [ ] softball
- [ ] basketball

What others? _____

_____

What are all the things you need to win?

- [ ] patience
- [ ] speed
- [ ] strong arms
- [ ] power
- [ ] bravery
- [ ] luck

- [ ] desire to win
- [ ] quick turns
- [ ] strength
- [ ] practice
- [ ] strong legs
- [ ] brains
- [ ] courage

What else? _____

_____

_____

These are the same things you can use to help you feel strong and safe now.

If you could change one
thing in your life, what
would it be and how
would you change it?

Write a
story with
a happy
ending.

Make three wishes
for yourself and
the world.

PLEASE READ THIS...

This is a brief guide to the design and use of the Growth and Recovery (GROW) workbooks from Hunter House. It is excerpted from detailed guidelines that can be downloaded from www .hunterhouse.com or are available free through the mail by calling the ordering number at the bottom of the page. Please consult the detailed guidelines before using this workbook for the first time.

GROW workbooks provide a way to open up communication with children who are not able to or who are reluctant to talk about a traumatic experience. They are not self-help books and are not designed for guardians or parents to use on their own with children. They address sensitive issues, and a child's recovery and healing require the safety, structured approach, and insight provided by a trained professional.

Each therapist will bring her own originality, creativity, and experience to the interaction and may adapt the tasks and activities in the workbooks, using other materials and activities. With less verbally oriented children, the use of art therapy or music or video may be recommended, or certain exercises may be conducted in groups.

Each pair of facing pages in the workbook provides the focus for a therapeutic "movement" that may take up one session. However, more than one movement can be made in a single session or several sessions may be devoted to a single movement. Children should be allowed to move through the process at their own pace. If a child finds a task too "hot" to approach, the therapist can return to it later. When something is fruitful it can be pursued with extended tasks.

While a therapist is free to select the order of activities for each child, the exercises are laid out in a progression based on the principles of critical incident stress management:

- initial exercises focus on building the therapeutic alliance
- the child is then led to relate an overview of the experience
- this is deepened by a "sensory-unpacking" designed to access and recover traumatic memories
- family experiences and changed living conditions, if any, are explored
- emotions are encouraged, explored, and validated.
- delayed reactions are dealt with, and resources are explored.
- the experience is integrated into the child's life through a series of strength-building exercises.

Specific pages in the GROW workbooks are cross-referenced to Dr. Kendall Johnson's book *Trauma in the Lives of Children* (Hunter House, Alameda, 1998). This provides additional information on the treatment of traumatized children.

The content of the workbooks should be shared with parents or significant adults only when the child feels ready for it and if it is therapeutically wise. Workbooks should not be given to children to take home until the therapeutic process is completed according to the therapist's satisfaction.

Although this series of workbooks was written for school-age children, the tasks are adaptable for use with younger children and adolescents.

Detailed guidelines are available for each GROW workbook (see list on front inside cover).

Printed in the USA
CPSIA information can be obtained
at www.ICGtesting.com
JSHW060049150824
68134JS00031B/2694